S. Hrg. 114–218

UNITED STATES SECURITY POLICY IN EUROPE

HEARING

BEFORE THE

COMMITTEE ON ARMED SERVICES
UNITED STATES SENATE

ONE HUNDRED FOURTEENTH CONGRESS

FIRST SESSION

APRIL 28, 2015

Printed for the use of the Committee on Armed Services

Available via the World Wide Web: http://www.fdsys.gov/

U.S. GOVERNMENT PUBLISHING OFFICE

99–668 PDF   WASHINGTON : 2016

For sale by the Superintendent of Documents, U.S. Government Publishing Office
Internet: bookstore.gpo.gov   Phone: toll free (866) 512–1800; DC area (202) 512–1800
Fax: (202) 512–2104   Mail: Stop IDCC, Washington, DC 20402–0001

COMMITTEE ON ARMED SERVICES

JOHN McCAIN, Arizona, *Chairman*

JAMES M. INHOFE, Oklahoma
JEFF SESSIONS, Alabama
ROGER F. WICKER, Mississippi
KELLY AYOTTE, New Hampshire
DEB FISCHER, Nebraska
TOM COTTON, Arkansas
MIKE ROUNDS, South Dakota
JONI ERNST, Iowa
THOM TILLIS, North Carolina
DAN SULLIVAN, Alaska
MIKE LEE, Utah
LINDSEY GRAHAM, South Carolina
TED CRUZ, Texas

JACK REED, Rhode Island
BILL NELSON, Florida
CLAIRE McCASKILL, Missouri
JOE MANCHIN III, West Virginia
JEANNE SHAHEEN, New Hampshire
KIRSTEN E. GILLIBRAND, New York
RICHARD BLUMENTHAL, Connecticut
JOE DONNELLY, Indiana
MAZIE K. HIRONO, Hawaii
TIM KAINE, Virginia
ANGUS S. KING, JR., Maine
MARTIN HEINRICH, New Mexico

CHRISTIAN D. BROSE, *Staff Director*
ELIZABETH L. KING, *Minority Staff Director*

(II)

CONTENTS

APRIL 28, 2015

(III)

UNITED STATES SECURITY POLICY IN EUROPE

TUESDAY, APRIL 28, 2015

U.S. SENATE,
COMMITTEE ON ARMED SERVICES,
Washington, DC.

The committee met, pursuant to notice, at 9:06 a.m., in SD–G50, Dirksen Senate Office Building, Senator John McCain (chairman) presiding.

Committee members present: Senators McCain, Inhofe, Ayotte, Rounds, Ernst, Tillis, Reed, Nelson, Manchin, Shaheen, Gillibrand, Donnelly, Hirono, Kaine, King, and Heinrich.

OPENING STATEMENT OF SENATOR JOHN McCAIN, CHAIRMAN

Chairman McCAIN. Well, good morning. This committee meets a little earlier than usual today since we have a briefing at 11 a.m. today on the recent unfortunate tragedy of the deaths of an American and another one in a drone strike. The committee meets today to receive testimony on U.S. security policy in Europe. I would like to thank each of our witnesses for appearing before us.

Admiral James Stavridis, dean of the Fletcher School of Law and Diplomacy at Tufts University and former Supreme Allied Commander, Europe; Ian Brzezinski, resident senior fellow at the Scowcroft Center at the Atlantic Council; and Stephen Sestanovich, the George Kennen senior fellow for Russian and Eurasian Studies at the Council on Foreign Relations.

Just like the United States, Europe confronts a diverse and complex array of crises that are making the world a more dangerous place. Already this year radical Islamists attacked Paris and Copenhagen. Last week in the Mediterranean, over 700 migrants perished tragically in a shipwreck fleeing the conflict and instability of North Africa. Then there is Russia. In 2012, the Defense Strategic Guidance argued that the changing global security environment offered a chance to rebalance the U.S. military investment in Europe while building a closer relationship with Russia.

The Obama administration eliminated two heavy brigades stationed in Europe and pursued a so-called reset policy towards Russia. Two years later, Russia's invasion and dismemberment of Ukraine should remind everyone of the true nature of Putin's ambitions and the fragility of peace in Europe. Since the end of the Cold War, U.S. policy toward Russia was based on a bipartisan assumption that the Russian government sought to integrate peacefully into the international order in Europe and to forego a constructive relationship with the United States based on mutual national interests.

The events of this past year have overturned that assumption. For the first time in 7 decades on the European continent, a state has sent its military forces across an internationally recognized border and forcibly annexed the sovereign territory of another state. Now, American strategy must adjust to the reality of the revisionist Russia that is undergoing a significant military modernization, and that is willing to use force not only as a last resort, but as a primary tool to achieve its neo-imperial objectives. In Ukraine, Russia has continued to violate the February ceasefire agreement. In fact, news today indicates an increase in the conflict. Rather than comply and withdraw from Ukraine, President Putin has maintained sizable numbers of artillery pieces and multiple rocket launchers in Ukraine.

According to the State Department, the Russian military has deployed additional air defense systems near the front lines in Eastern Ukraine, the highest amount since last August, and a disturbing sign that another offensive may be imminent. In response, it is not that the United States and our European allies have done nothing. It is that nothing we have done has succeeded in deterring Putin's aggression and halted his slow motion annexation of Eastern Ukraine.

The Ukrainian people do not want U.S. or western troops to fight for them. They are simply asking for the right tools to defend themselves and their country. Senator Reed and I, along with members of this committee on both sides of the aisle, have called on the administration to provide defensive lethal assistance to Ukraine. Unfortunately, the President's continued inaction incredibly for fear of provoking Russia is seen by Putin as weakness and invites the very aggression we seek to avoid.

Of course there is no military solution in Ukraine, but there is a clear military dimension to achieving a political solution. As three major think tanks wrote recently, "Assisting Ukraine to deter attack and defend itself is not inconsistent with the search for a peaceful political solution. It is essential to achieving it." Only if the Kremlin knows that the risks and costs of further military action are high will it seek to find an acceptable political solution. The failure to raise the cost of Putin's aggression in Ukraine only increases and makes it more likely that this aggression could expand to places like Moldova, Georgia, the Baltic States, and Central Asia.

This is even more worrisome in light of Russia's increasing emphasis on nuclear weapons. Putin has personally presided over nuclear weapons drills in recent months, deployed Icelander missiles to Kaliningrad capable of carrying nuclear warheads and claiming the right to deploy nuclear weapons on the Crimean peninsula. Russia continues to violate the IMF [Intermediate-Range Nuclear Forces] treaty as nuclear weapons become more prominent in its military doctrine.

Equally concerning, Russia's military buildup also appears designed to deny the United States and NATO [North Atlantic Treaty Organization] access to key parts of Europe, especially the Baltic and Black Sea regions, as a way of trying to make U.S. security commitments to our allies too costly to fulfill. Russia is clearly learning from China in this regard.

Russia's intensifying military activity in contempt of international law also extends to the Arctic where it has stood up a new military command with more troops and aircraft military infrastructure and increased military exercises. One exercise last month included nearly 40,000 troops and more than 55 ships and submarines. The administration needs to address this problem as the United States assumes the chairmanship of the Arctic Council over the next 2 years.

In response to the broader challenge that Russia poses to security in Europe hereto, it is not that the United States and NATO have done nothing. We have created a modest rapid reaction force, increased air policing and sea patrols, expanded training and exercises, and deployed small numbers of additional forces to Estonia, Latvia, Lithuania, and Poland. The problem is the actions we have taken seem inadequate to the scope, scale, and seriousness of the challenges we face.

I would especially highlight the fact that too many of our NATO allies continue to fail to provide for their own defense despite promises at the Wales Summit to ''reverse the trend of declining defense budget.'' Soon Poland and Estonia may be the only other allies meeting our alliance's commitment to spend 2 percent of GDP on defense.

None of us want to return to the Cold War, but we need to face the reality that we are dealing with a Russian ruler who wants exactly that, especially as a way of enhancing Russian relevance amid systemic demographic collapse and economic crisis. The reason for maintaining a strong U.S. military presence in Europe is the same as ever. To deter conflict and aggression, we must forget this lesson at our peril. Ultimately, we must lift our sights and recognize that we are facing the reality of a challenge that many had assumed was resigned to the history books: a strong militarily capable state that is hostile to our interests and our values and seeks to overturn the international order in Europe that American leaders of both parties have sought to maintain since World War II.

I hope today's hearings will help us to better understand the magnitude of this challenge and what to do about it. I thank each of our witnesses for joining us today, and I look forward to their testimony. I would note in the audience we have parliamentarians from Ukraine, Kosovo, and Nepal who are with us today. I welcome them to our hearing. I especially want to express my appreciation for our legislators from Ukraine who are here on behalf of their country.

Senator Reed?

STATEMENT OF SENATOR JACK REED

Senator REED. Thank you very much, Mr. Chairman, and thank you, gentlemen, Admiral Stavridis, Mr. Brzezinski, and Dr. Sestanovich, welcome. Let me thank the chairman for setting up this hearing to review the security situation in Europe. It will inform our upcoming deliberations on the annual defense authorization bill. On Thursday we will hear from General Breedlove, the Commander of U.S. European Command and NATO Supreme Allied Commander, and this hearing will be a wonderful way to begin that discussion with General Breedlove.

The transatlantic relationship remains central to the United States and global security. Our NATO allies and European partners have been the primary contributors to the United States-led coalition operations in the Middle East and South Asia. In Afghanistan, European countries have deployed more than 260,000 personnel since 2007, accounting for more than 90 percent of the non-U.S. forces participating in the ISAF [International Security Assistance Force] mission that ended last December.

Today, however, our European partners face security challenges closer to home. As noted at the NATO Summit in Wales last September, Russia's aggression against Ukraine has challenged the alliance's vision of a Europe whole, free, and at peace. Russia has engaged in hybrid warfare to seize Crimea and back separatist forces in Eastern Ukraine in violation of the ceasefire agreement signed in September of last year and this February. According to the U.S. and military leaders, Russia continues to flow heavy weapons and equipment into the separatist areas, sparking fears of renewed heavy fighting within the coming weeks.

One step this committee and Congress have supported is providing Ukraine the military assistance, including defense weapons, necessary for it to defend itself against further attacks. A recent report by leading think tanks, which Dr. Sestanovich co-authored, argues that ''Assisting Ukraine to deter attack and defend itself is not inconsistent with the search for a peaceful political solution. It is essential to achieving it.''

I hope our witnesses will address whether they believe there is a coalition of countries willing to provide assistance to Ukraine, and whether preparing such a coalition effort would help or harm compliance with the ceasefire agreements. At the NATO Wales Summit, members approved a Readiness Action Plan to enhance the alliance's ability to respond quickly to security challenges. This year's budget request includes $800 million on top of the $1 billion approved last year for the European Reassurance Initiative, to enhance the United States' military presence and activities in Europe.

A key issue over the coming years will be how U.S. forces should be postured in Europe to reassure allies and provide for a collective defense. This will depend in part on whether our NATO allies live up to their pledges on defense spending and the levels of host nation support for U.S. forces in Europe.

NATO is facing security challenges along its other borders as well. Countries along the Mediterranean border are grappling with the prospect of tens of thousands, possibly more, of migrants fleeing instability in Libya, Syria, Eritrea, and elsewhere. Efforts to respond to this crisis have been mixed to date, and it is clear more must be done soon because the flow of migrants is not likely to subside given increasing violence in Libya and other conflict zones.

To the southeast, the flow of foreign fighters across Turkey's border into Syria and back heightens the risk of future anti-western attacks like those in Paris and Brussels, and raises the question as to whether ISIL [the Islamic State of Iraq and the Levant] has more broadly infiltrated Europe's cities. In the north, Russia is expanding its military activities in the Arctic, potentially challenging international norms and laws governing that region.

I look forward to our witnesses' testimony on these and other security challenges in Europe, and, again, I thank them for their willingness to appear this morning. Thank you.

Chairman MCCAIN. I welcome the witnesses. Admiral Stavridis?

STATEMENT OF ADM JAMES G. STAVRIDIS, USN [RET.], DEAN OF THE FLETCHER SCHOOL OF LAW AND DIPLOMACY, TUFTS UNIVERSITY, MEDFORD, MA

Admiral STAVRIDIS. Chairman McCain, Ranking Member Reed, members of the committee, it is a delight to be back with you. Last time I was dressed somewhat more glamorously than I am today. It is a pleasure to share some ideas and thoughts on the situation in Europe, which have, as we heard in those statements from the chairman and the ranking member, have taken a turn for the worse in a security dimension over the last 24 months since I left my post as the Supreme Allied Commander.

I want to just begin by saying, why does Europe matter? I get that question. Does Europe really matter for the United States? We talk a lot about a pivot to the Pacific and so on, and we should globally. But I would argue Europe matters for a wide variety of reasons.

First and foremost, we share enormous values, our values: democracy, liberty, freedom of speech, freedom of religion. These come from Europe, from the Enlightenment. Second, NATO, this alliance, 28 nations, 52 percent of the world's GDP, 3 million men and women under arms, almost all of them volunteers, 24,000 military aircraft. This is a terrific partner for the United States in Europe. Third, the bases. Sometimes people will say, oh, those are Cold War bases. Not so in my view. These are forward-operating stations of the 21st century. We need them to move our forces into Africa, into the Levant, into the Middle East, into Central Asia. They are irreplaceable.

Fourth, the economy. The largest trade flow in the world goes across the Atlantic. It is about $5 trillion. So, this economic bridge across the Atlantic is of enormous importance to us. Then finally, as we look at Europe, it is a place full of high tech, of well-trained military. It is a wealth of resources. So for all those reasons, Europe matters.

I think the challenges were well laid out by the chairman and the ranking member. It is Russia which has invaded a nation and annexed its territory. We cannot understate the gravity of that experience, and we should not understate how that ghost rattles through the Europe zeitgeist.

The ranking member, I think, correctly drew a line under ISIS [the Islamic State of Iraq and Syria] and its threat to Europe. I am deeply concerned about it not only across the NATO borders in Turkey, but across the sea routes from Italy. Last year, some 200,000 migrants; this year on track to double that. Within those numbers will be some group of violent extremists, Islamic radicals who come to strike at highly symbolic targets, probably starting in Italy. The Arctic was well covered by the opening statements.

I would add only the Balkans, which we tend not to think about a great deal these days. They were a place of great tension and danger 15 years ago, yet today tensions continue in Kosovo, across its borders to Serbia, and, most notably, in Bosnia, a very fragile tripartite structure. Yesterday Muslim extremist terrorists struck in the Serbian portions of Bosnia. That is still a place where we need to keep a weather eye.

So I will close by saying as we look at all this, our own U.S. security presence in Europe is diminished greatly, certainly since the end of the Cold War. We are down 75 percent in personnel. We are down 75 percent in the number of bases that we have. We have, in my view, come to a line that we should not continue to diminish that presence further. I would argue in the end we need to stay engaged in Europe for the reasons about which I have spoken as well as for the challenges so well articulated by the chairman and the ranking member.

Thank you.

Chairman McCAIN. Thank you. Mr. Brzezinski?

STATEMENT OF IAN J. BRZEZINSKI, RESIDENT SENIOR FELLOW, BRENT SCOWCROFT CENTER ON INTERNATIONAL SECURITY, ATLANTIC COUNCIL, WASHINGTON, DC

Mr. BRZEZINSKI. Thank you, Chairman McCain, thank you, Ranking Member Reed, members of the committee. I really appreciate this opportunity to participate in this hearing on the state of U.S. security interests in Europe.

NATO is the institutional cornerstone of transatlantic security, and today that alliance faces challenges on multiple fronts of unprecedented complexity and increasing urgency. To the east, Europe confronts Russia's invasion of Ukraine and increasingly provocative military conduct across the region. To its north, the transatlantic community faces Russia's militarization of the Arctic, a region rich in resources, but also of contested sovereignty. To its south, the alliance faces a treacherous combination of state sponsors of terrorism, failed states, and extremist organizations in an arc stretching from the Middle East across North Africa. ISIS atrocities and refugee flows to Europe are tragic manifestations of that front.

In an age of globalization, NATO cannot afford to be a regionally focused alliance. It must address a global front. It must remain prepared and ready to take on challenges well beyond the North Atlantic area in a world that is increasingly interconnected and volatile.

Allow me to focus my remarks on the first front, a sort of returning back to the future driven by Russia's confrontational approach toward the west. Putin's invasion of Ukraine has disrupted the order that has kept peace in Europe since World War II. It is a direct threat to the credibility of NATO and the vision of a Europe whole, free, and secure. It is but one element of a revanchist policy intended to reestablish Russian hegemony, if not full control, over space akin to the former Soviet Union.

Toward this end, Moscow has applied the full suite of Russian power to weaken and dominate its neighbors: military force, economic and energy embargos, political subterfuge, information and cyber warfare, separatist groups, and frozen conflicts. The campaign history includes Moscow's attempt to subvert the 2004 Ukraine Orange Revolution, its 2007 cyberattack on Estonia, and the 2008 invasion of Georgia.

It is a campaign that pursues 20th century objectives leveraging 21st century techniques, and old-fashioned brute force. It rests on a $750 billion defense modernization plan that is upgrading Russian conventional and nuclear forces. It is a strategy that involves provocative military actions beyond Ukraine intended to intimidate, divide, and test the capabilities of members and partners of the NATO alliance. You know well these actions: the increase in assertive naval and air patrols; violations of allied and partner sea, air, and ground space; harassment of military and civilian aircraft and ships; and a steady stream of nuclear threats from Russian officials, including President Putin himself.

Russian military exercises have been an important part of these shows of force. They are notable for their magnitude and the frequency of spot exercises, sudden and unannounced mobilization deployment of forces. As indicated in the attached chart and the ones I think are in the testimony I submitted, over the last 3 years Russia has conducted at least 6 major military exercises, and these have ranged from 65,000 personnel to 165,000 personnel. They dwarf in comparison to the size of NATO exercises, and raise in my mind questions about the alliance's political and operational ability to mobilize comparable forces.

The west's response to Russia's military assertiveness has consisted of limited, incremental escalations of economic sanctions and military deployments. This incrementalism conveys hesitancy and the lack of unity and determination. It has failed to convince Putin to reverse course. Indeed, it may have actually emboldened him. For these reasons, continued incrementalism not only promises continued conflict in Ukraine, but also an increased danger of wider war.

This is underscored when one considers what will be the likely state of Ukraine and Russia if the west holds to its current policies. Where will Ukraine be in 6 to 12 months? It is likely to experience a further loss of territory. Its economy will be further crippled. Its population and government will be at risk of being more disillusioned. This is a Ukraine more vulnerable and more enticing to Putin's revanchist ambitions.

Where will Russia be in 6 to 12 months? Its economy will likely be somewhat weaker, its leaders marginally more internationally isolated. Under such circumstances, President Putin can be expected to be more irrationally nationalist and more brazen. That is a Russia more likely to attempt incursions further into Ukraine and escalate its provocative military actions against the west. Under such a scenario, not only are Ukraine's prospects more dire, the prospects of a collision, albeit inadvertent, between Russian and western forces are increased. The very risk of conflict escalation that current policy has been designed to avert will actually be more likely.

Calibrated engagement with the Russian government is needed to explore avenues by which to modulate tensions and to return to Ukraine's territories. However, to be effective these efforts will require more immediate and longer-term initiatives that will impose higher economic costs on Moscow, deter it from further provocative conduct, and reinforce the security of Central Europe. Toward these ends, I recommended that U.S. policy aim to do the following. First, we should impose stronger economic sanctions on Russia. Sectorial sanctions are needed to more aggressively shock the Russian economy by shutting off its energy and financial sectors from the global economy.

Second, the alliance should do more to reinforce NATO's eastern frontier. I believe the alliance should station a brigade-level combat capability permanently in Poland and Romania. It should station battalion-level capabilities in each of the Baltic states, and it should provide NATO's military commander, SACEUR [the Supreme Allied Commander Europe], the authorities necessary to deploy forces in real time in response to provocative military actions. NATO has never responded to any of the exercises and provocative actions I mentioned. It has been passive.

More has to be done to reinforce Kiev's capability for self-defense. The deployment of U.S. and allied military trainers is a good step that occurred this last month, but it is overdue. The west should also arm Ukraine with air defense and anti-tank weapons and other capabilities it has been requesting so it can better defend itself. The west should deploy intelligence and surveillance capacities to Ukraine to enhance Ukraine's situational awareness, and it should conduct military exercises in Ukraine just as EUCOM [United States European Command] did last summer to help train Ukraine's armed forces, and to demonstrate the west's solidarity with Ukraine.

None of these recommendations present a territorial threat to Russia. They would help erase the red line the west has allowed Russia to redraw in Europe. They would present Moscow the possibility of a costly and prolonged military conflict. Let me add, the United States should be also front and center with the Europeans in the negotiations addressing Russia's invasion of Ukraine. Washington's absence from the Minsk process is a clear opportunity cost in the effort to bring this conflict to a peaceful and just end.

Fourth, similar security assistance should be offered to other countries threatened by the shadow of Putin's assertive policies. Here I am thinking particularly of Moldova and especially of Georgia because of its strategic location. Finally, the west needs to reanimate the vision of a Europe whole and free. Because of NATO enlargement, Europe has been better able to manage the aggression the continent has experienced over the last year. We need to ensure the alliance's open door policy has not devolved into a passive phrase or empty slogan.

Let me close by a simple point—with a simple point. The most effective way to counter hegemonic aspirations is to deny them the opportunity for actualization. Security in Central Europe is critical not only for peace in Europe, it is also a key element of an effective strategy to forge a normal relationship, if not eventually a partnership, with Russia.

Thank you.

[The prepared statement of Mr. Brzezinski follows:]

Chairman McCain, Ranking Member Reed, Members of the Committee, I am honored to speak at this hearing on the state of U.S. security interests in Europe.

We meet today some eight months after the September 4, 2014 NATO summit in Wales, United Kingdom. That meeting of Allied heads of state proved to be an important inflection point for the Alliance. When planning for that summit began, its primary objective was to mark the end of NATO's combat operations in Afghanistan. Some were even concerned about the future relevance of NATO, anticipating that it was about to enter a period of unprecedented operational inactivity following decades of defending against the Soviet Union, managing conflict in the Balkans, and, more recently, contributing to out-of area undertakings in Afghanistan and even Iraq.

Instead, the Alliance's agenda that Fall was dominated by events that most policy-makers on both sides of the Atlantic failed to anticipate. These, of course, include Russia's invasion of Ukraine and the sudden and bloodthirsty rise of ISIS in Syria and Iraq.

A read of the summit communiqué reflects other challenges confronting the Alliance: missile proliferation, chaos in Libya, crises in Mali and the Congo African Republic, threats to the global commons—including its cyber and maritime domains, and Iran's nuclear program, among others.

That list gives real credence to former NATO Secretary General Fogh Rasmussen's repeated assertions that we face a more connected, more complex, more chaotic and more precarious world. He is right. In this world, the political and military capacities that NATO can leverage has become only more vital to the shared interests and values that define the transatlantic community.

I would like today to focus on four urgent and emergent fronts before the NATO Alliance:

- An Eastern Front driven by a Russia's provocative military actions;
- An emergent Arctic Front driven by Moscow's militarization of the High North;
- A Southern Front, a region stretching from Iran across the Middle East and North Africa wrought by a dangerous combination of failed states and extremist organizations; and,
- A Global Front defined by the upheaval generated by the rapidly evolving dynamics of globalization.

THE EASTERN FRONT: RUSSIA'S INVASION OF UKRAINE

Let me start with the front that is sort of a return back to the future. Fourteen months ago, President Putin launched his invasion of Ukraine with the incursion of 20–30,000 Russian troops into the Crimean peninsula. That was followed by the cross-border operation into Eastern Ukraine involving Russian provocateurs and Special Forces who seized buildings and armories and terrorized the local population. The latter were soon reinforced by Russian conventional forces. Both operations were backed by the massing of Russian conventional forces on Ukraine' border, under the guise of a 150,000 man military exercise.

Russia's invasion caused over 6000 Ukrainians deaths in eastern Ukraine and displaced over 1.6M people. More than 20% of Ukraine's industrial capability has been seized or destroyed. Crimea and regions of Donetsk and Luhansk remain occupied and are being politically purged. Russia is reinforcing its presence in Crimea with Special Forces, aircraft, and ships and has announced plans to deploy nuclear capable SS–26 Iskander missiles. In Eastern Ukraine where fighting continues, Putin violates the Minsk II peace accords by deploying additional heavy combat equipment, personnel and military supplies to his forces.

Russia's aggression against Ukraine presents a significant challenge to the security and stability of Europe and to the credibility of NATO. As an unprovoked aggression against the territorial sovereignty of a European nation, the invasion of Ukraine disrupts the order that has kept peace in Europe since World War II. By asserting the unilateral right to redraw borders on the grounds he is protecting ethnic Russians and by promoting the concept of a "Novorossiya," Putin has reintroduced the principal of ethnic sovereignty, a principal that wrought death and destruction across Europe in the last century and those before.

Putin's invasion of Ukraine, one motivated significantly by his opposition to the country's long-standing desire to be a fully integrated part of Europe, is a direct threat to the vision of a Europe whole, free and secure. If allowed to succeed, Putin's invasion of Ukraine will create a new confrontational divide in Europe, between a community defined by self-determination, democracy, and rule of law and one burdened by authoritarianism, hegemony and occupation. In these ways, Putin's aggression against Ukraine – and his increasingly provocative military actions elsewhere in Europe – are direct challenges to NATO and U.S. leadership, ones intended to portray the Alliance and Washington as lacking the diplomatic, economic, and military capacity to counter Russian power.

Putin's Revanchist Ambitions: The invasion of Ukraine is but one element of a revanchist policy that President Putin has articulated and exercised since taking office in 1999. His objective has been to reestablish Russian hegemony, if not full control, over the space of the former Soviet Union.

Toward this end, Moscow has applied the full suite of Russian power to weaken and dominate its neighbors: economic embargoes, political subterfuge, information and cyber-warfare, separatist groups, frozen conflicts as well as military shows of force and incursions. Putin's campaign history includes Moscow's attempt to subvert Ukraine's 2004 Orange Revolution, the 2007 cyber attack against Estonia, the separatist movement in Moldova, energy embargoes against Lithuania and Ukraine, and the 2008 invasion of Georgia.

President Putin's strategy is one that pursues 20th-century objectives through 21st-century techniques and old-fashioned brute force. With regard to the latter, Russia has undertaken a determined modernization of its armed forces. Some $750B has been dedicated over this decade to expand the Russian fleet, introduce 5th generation aircraft, deploy new missiles, modernize his nuclear arsenal, increase his nation's SOF capabilities, and militarize the Arctic. When one compares the Russian forces that invaded Georgia in 2008 to those that led the invasion of Crimea last year, the modernization campaign is clearly yielding improved capabilities.

As part of his strategy, Putin has deployed his military forces in provocative ways across the Baltic region, the Black Sea, the Arctic and elsewhere to demonstrate capability, intimidate and divide Russia's neighbors, and probe the resolve of the West. These actions have steadily escalated over time, and include challenges to the airspace of Sweden, the cross-border seizure of an Estonian law-enforcement officer, harassment of military and civilian aircraft and ships in the Baltic and Black Seas, and an exponential increase in assertive air and sea patrols by Russian aircraft and ships on both sides of the Atlantic.

Russian military exercises have been an important part of these shows of force and are notable for their magnitude and for the frequency of ''spot'' exercises – the sudden and unannounced mobilization and deployment of forces. As indicated in the attached chart, over the last three years, Russia has conducted at six major military exercises involving between 65,000 and 160,000 personnel. In comparison, these dwarf the size of NATO and Allied exercises, and raise questions about the Alliance's comparable ability to mobilize comparable forces in no-notice situations.

Russia's assertive military conduct has been complemented by an increase in nuclear threats against the West made by senior Russian commanders and civilian officials, including President Putin. In the last several weeks, Moscow threatened to target Romania, Poland and Denmark with nuclear weapons for their contributions to transatlantic missile defense. *The Times* of London recently reported that in a meeting with U.S. officials, Russian generals threatened ''a spectrum of responses from nuclear to non-military'' if the Alliance deployed additional forces to the Baltic states.

The West's Response: To date, the West's response to Russia's territorial aggression and provocative military actions consists of limited incremental escalations of economic sanctions and military deployments. The failure of this response to convince Putin to reverse course is rooted in this incrementalism which communicates hesitancy and a lack of unity and determination. Indeed, it may have actually emboldened Putin. Today, Moscow's provocative exercises and assertive military conduct continue, Crimea and Eastern Ukraine remain occupied, and Russia's forces appear poised to strike deeper into Ukraine.

Calibrated engagement with the Russian government is needed to explore avenues by which to modulate tensions and return to Ukraine its territories. However, to be effective these efforts will require more immediate and longer-term initiatives that will impose economic costs on Russia, deter Moscow from further provocative conduct, reinforce Central and Eastern Europe's sense of security, enhance Ukraine's capacity for defense, and help it transform into a successful, democratic, and prosperous European state. These include:

1) **Stronger economic sanctions on Russia.** The current approach of targeting specific Russian individuals and companies has not changed Putin's course of action, not is it likely to do so. Russia is a country that rightfully takes great pride in its history of enduring economic and military hardship. An authoritarian regime will always be more resistant to economic sanctions than a democratic system. Sectoral sanctions are needed to more aggressively shock the Russian economy by shutting off its energy and financial sectors from the global economy.

2) **Stronger reinforcement of NATO's eastern frontier.** Russia repeatedly mobilized ten of thousands of troops for its invasion of Ukraine and in its shows of force. NATO's response has been far more limited, involving dozens of aircraft, company level deployments (and the occasional battalion) and a few ships. The gap is noticeable to Putin, our Allies and our partners. The Alliance should:

- Base a brigade level combat capability permanently to Poland and Romania;
- Base battalion level capacities to each of the Baltic states;
- Provide NATO's top military commander, the Supreme Allied Commander Europe, authorities necessary to deploy forces in real time against provocative Russian military operations; and,
- Expand the mission of NATO missile defense and the U.S. European Phased Adaptive Approach (EPAA) to address the threat posed by Russian ballistic missiles

3) **Military Assistance to Ukraine:** Greater effort must be made to reinforce Ukraine's capability for self-defense. By denying Kyiv's request for needed military weapons, the West not only precludes Ukraine the ability to better defend itself, it is de facto accepting Putin's effort to draw a new red line in Europe, allowing the reemergence of a grey zone in Europe.

This has been deeply disillusioning for Ukrainians who so courageously expressed their desire on the Maidan for freedom and a place in Europe. It threatens to shatter the bipartisan/transatlantic vision of a Europe whole, free and undivided that has guided U.S. and European security policy for the last 25 years.

The United States and other keys allies are to be commended for the long-overdue step of deploying military trainers to Ukraine, but they should also:

- Provide military equipment to Ukraine, including air defense and anti-tank weapons as well as key enablers, such as drones, that would enhance Ukraine's ability to leverage the capabilities of its armed forces
- Deploy intelligence and surveillance capabilities
- Conduct military exercises in Ukraine, as EUCOM did in the Summer of 2014, to help train Ukraine's armed forces and to demonstrate solidarity with Ukraine

None of these recommendations would present a territorial threat to Russia, but they would complicate Putin's ambitions regarding Ukraine. They would help erase the red line that Moscow has been allowed to redraw in Europe. They would assure Ukrainians that they are not alone and demonstrate that Putin is unable to intimidate the West. They would present Moscow the possibility of a costly and prolonged military conflict.

The United States should also be front and center with the Europeans in the negotiations addressing Russia's aggression against Ukraine. The absence of the United States at the negotiating table signals a lack of commitment to European security and thus devalues the presentation of transatlantic solidarity against this invasion. It has been an opportunity cost to the effort to bring this conflict to peaceful and just end.

4) **Support to Ukraine's economic transformation.** In this regard, the United States and the West has been constructive, providing significant EU, IMF, and bilateral economic assistance packages. However, the goals of such economic assistance are difficult if not impossible to realize when Ukraine is subject to a violent invasion as well as to political, economic and other pressures from Russia.

5) **A Reanimation of the Vision of Europe Whole and Free:** For much of the post-Cold War period, U.S. policy was clearly guided by the vision of a Europe, undivided, secure, and free. For over two decades, Washington wisely supported the indigenous ambitions of Central European democracies for membership in NATO and the European Union. Those processes of enlargement have benefited all parties in Europe, expanding the zone of peace, stability, and prosperity across the continent.

The United States needs to reanimate the process of NATO enlargement, making clear that the Alliance's ''open-door policy'' for membership is no passive phrase or empty slogan. Doing so would be an important way to underscore Washington's commitment to the security of Central and Eastern Europe. For these reasons, no decision or recommendation should be permitted or advanced that would in any way limit its applicability to any country of Europe, including Ukraine.

The Risks of Incrementalism: There are real risks that flow from the West's current strategy of incrementalism against President Putin's aggression: Continued incrementalism not only promises continued conflict in Ukraine but also an increased danger of wider war.

This is underscored when one considers what will be the likely state of Ukraine and Russia if the West holds to its current course.

What will be the state of Ukraine in 6–18 months? It is likely to experience a further loss of territory. Its economy will be further crippled, thereby rendering the nation less able undertake reform. Its population is at risk of being more disillusioned, and government consequently weaker, if not divided. That is a Ukraine more vulnerable and more enticing to Putin's revanchist ambitions.

What will be the state of Russia in 6–18 months? Its economy will likely be somewhat weaker, if it is not bolstered by a rise in energy prices. It may be marginally more isolated. Under such circumstances, President Putin can be expected to be more irrationally nationalistic and more brazen. That is a Russia more likely to attempt incursions further into Ukraine and escalate its provocative military actions against the West.

Under such a scenario, not only are Ukraine's prospects more dire, the prospects of collision, albeit inadvertent, between Russian and Western forces are increased. The very risk of conflict escalation that the current policy has been designed to avert will be more likely.

THE ARTIC: AN EMERGING FRONT

The resource rich Arctic has become a high priority of President Putin's security policy. Russia's ensuing militarization of the High North has made it an emergent front affecting transatlantic security.

Moscow has established an Arctic Military command backed by a joint Arctic task force. It has re-opened Cold War naval and air bases and is building a string of new military facilities across the Arctic. It is reinforcing the Northern Fleet with more ice-breakers, surface combatants and submarines. Russia has stepped-up Cold War military operations in the region, including the testing of missiles and aggressive naval and air patrols that prod the territories of the U.S. and other allies.

Enhancing NATO's role in the Arctic: If the High North is to remain a zone defined by peace and stability, the West will have to introduce a more robust security dimension into its Arctic policies, and a centerpiece of that effort should include a greater role for NATO. Indeed, as more non-Arctic nations start to operate in the Arctic, it will be useful to leverage the geopolitical weight that comes with a community of like-minded North Atlantic democracies.

NATO should expand its political and operational role in the Arctic, leveraging its maritime and air capacities. The Alliance can serve as a useful vehicle to coordinate and execute Arctic security cooperation, including intelligence exchanges, surveillance operations, military training and exercises, air policing, and disaster response. It can also foster the development of capabilities necessary for Arctic operations.

In these ways, NATO can fill a security gap that exists in the Arctic and do so without undermine existing useful institutions like the Arctic Council. This does not preclude Arctic cooperation with Moscow, particularly in areas such as search and rescue and disaster response. Indeed, the region can serve as an avenue of mutually beneficial engagement with Russia, even in this time of increased tension.

The bottom line is that if the Alliance plays a greater role in Arctic security today, the transatlantic community is going to be able to manage, if not prevent, a serious security crisis tomorrow.

THE SOUTHERN FRONT: FAILING STATES AND IDEOLOGICAL UPHEAVAL

NATO faces a Southern front—an arc of instability stretching from Iran to the shores of North Africa. It is a realm in which societal upheavals and regional power struggles have generated challenges of varying levels of urgency—from Tehran's nuclear programs, to the chaos traumatizing Syria and Iraq to the tragic flood of refuges flowing to Europe from Africa and Middle East.

Among the more urgent of these crises lies south of Turkey, caused by the sudden and savage rise of ISIS in Syria and Iraq. Because of the links of ISIS and other violent groups in this region to Europe and North America, this is an urgent threat to transatlantic security. The West's goal must be more than the degradation or destruction of ISIS and other like-minded groups. It must be the prevention of Iraq, Syria and other areas from serving as havens and breeding grounds for such extremism. That is going to require a comprehensive, long-term strategy that will require considerable military, economic and political resources.

That response will have to be a multi-lateral undertaking and not just transatlantic undertaking. It must executed in partnership with key powers of the Muslim world—Turkey, of course, but also Jordan, Egypt and Saudi Arabia, in addition to Iraq and moderate elements within Syria. It should leverage the various capacities of NATO, the European Union, the Gulf Cooperation Council, and the Arab League, among others. Only then will one be able to leverage the cumulative strengths of the West and mitigate the historic baggage many Allies have in the region.

It will require sustained military action and security assistance. The tip of the spear addressing threats like ISIS has to be local forces. The Iraqi security forces, the Peshmerga, and moderate Syrian factions stand among these elements, but they will need to be backed by foreign airpower, reinforced by foreign equipment, intelligence, combat advisors and trainers as well as special forces prepared for direct action.

The multi-lateral effort will require significant humanitarian assistance. This is needed to assist not just those displaced in Iraq, but also to assist the governments of neighboring countries—particularly Turkey and Jordan—whose state structures and societies are at risk of being overburdened, if not destabilized, by refugees fleeing the region's violence.

The strategy will have to include a long-term effort to help enable the crippled states and societies of Europe's North African and the Middle Eastern periphery to benefit from economic growth and sound governance. Those are the most powerful weapons against extremism. Military strikes and humanitarian assistance may often be required, but they are tactical actions, necessary but not sufficient to tackle a strategic problem. Good governance and prosperity are ultimately the best ways to ensure that these societies do not serve as breeding grounds for extremism and terrorist recruits.

THE GLOBAL FRONT

These aforementioned three fronts to Europe's East, North and South are affected by a fourth NATO front—the front generated and sustained by the dynamics of globalization.

Globalization clearly has it is positive sides. Advances in transportation and communications have facilitated the spread of prosperity, respect for human rights, and democratic principles of governance, among other positive attributes of modernity.

However, these benefits have also been accompanied by challenges. The proliferation of weapons technologies and the emergence non-state actors with global reach—such as ISIS, al Qaeda and others—constitute some of the threats facilitated by globalization.

The profusion of communications technologies, a key dynamic of globalization, contributes to what Zbigniew Brzezinski (my father) calls a global political awakening that has been evident in the velvet revolutions of 1989, the orange revolution in Ukraine, and the Arab Spring.

Communication technologies are empowering societies in ways can bring down dictators, end corrupt autocracies, and create opportunities for democracy, reform and accountability in government. However, a political awakening can also be an impatient force, one prone to destructive violence when it is driven primarily by sentiments flowing from inequity and injustice and lacks leadership with a platform of clear objectives. In those cases, societies are often left vulnerable to organized groups leveraging dangerous ideologies.

Another key dynamic of globalization has been a profound shift in the global balance of power. A more complex constellation of actors with global reach and ambitions is emerging. These include China, India, and Brazil, and could well include others in the future.

As a result, we are entering a world where the predominance of the United States, even in collusion with Europe, is not what it was in the past. The emergence of new powers with regional, if not global, aspirations is often accompanied by territorial claims, historic grudges, and economic demands that can drive geopolitical tension, competition and collision.

Together these three dynamics increase the likelihood of regional conflicts. They make consensual decision-making more difficult among nation states, including within NATO, and they yield a world that is more volatile and unpredictable.

Many of these tensions and collisions are and will occur both near and far from the North Atlantic area, but in an age of globalization their economic and security implications can be immediate to both sides of the transatlantic community.

These global challenges make it all the more important for the transatlantic community to work together on all fronts. A vital underpinning of the NATO Alliance in this new century is the Transatlantic Bargain, one in which the United States sustains its commitment to European security and in return our Allies remain steadfast in their commitment to address with the United States threats and challenges that emanate from well beyond the North Atlantic area.

Protecting and promoting transatlantic security and values amidst these four NATO fronts—the East, the Arctic, the South and the challenges of global upheaval—stand among the defining challenges of our time. They present complex, long-term and costly undertakings that require:

- *Economic resources* that can be readily mobilized to in times of crisis and dedicated to economic development;
- *Military capabilities* that are expeditious and can be readily integrated with civilian efforts; and,
- *Political legitimacy* that is optimized through multilateral versus unilateral action.

In each of these requirements, the transatlantic community is preeminent. Its economies account for over 50% of the global GDP—some five times that of China and fourteen times that of Russia. Its military establishments are second to none, and NATO remains the worlds most successful and capable military Alliance

Above all, the transatlantic community presents a collective of likeminded democracies—and herein lies a vision for its role in the global order of today and tomorrow: NATO can and should serve as the core of a geographically and culturally expanding community of democracies that act collectively to promote freedom, stability and security around in what is an increasingly dynamic globalized environment. But it will require all of us to do more together.

Chairman MCCAIN. Thank you very much. Dr. Sestanovich?

STATEMENT OF STEPHEN SESTANOVICH, PH.D., GEORGE F. KENNAN SENIOR FELLOW FOR RUSSIAN AND EURASIAN STUDIES, COUNCIL ON FOREIGN RELATIONS

Dr. SESTANOVICH. Chairman McCain, Senator Reed, members of the committee, thank you for today's opportunity to join your discussion.

Admiral Stavridis gave a number of reasons why Europe matters. I agree with him. I would add one more: what it can contribute to the global balance of power. A united west can have more confidence in our ability to defend our interests worldwide. Divided we can be much less sure.

The past year has been a frustrating one for anyone trying to anticipate Russian moves. Time and again, many of us failed to gauge Vladimir Putin's motives. Often we thought he would be ready to unwind this crisis when he was just about to double down. He made promises that he did not keep and created a powerful case for western sanctions. Putin has personally antagonized American and European leaders in a manner that has few precedents in the history of Russia's relations with the west.

After a year like this, where do we stand and what should we think? I would like to focus on four issues that have produced considerable debate. They bear directly on choices that your committee must make. First is the question of Putin's aims and calculations; second is the effectiveness of sanctions; third is the question of helping the Ukraine military; and finally a fourth, fear of where this confrontation is heading. Many people worry that Putin will turn against neighbors especially our Baltic allies.

Our debate on all of these issues has brought many truths to the surface, but I think we have not got the whole story. To develop the right strategy, we need a fuller picture. First, on the nature of Putin's commitment to this—your phrase, Senator, was neo-imperialist policy. We should neither minimize nor exaggerate it. When separatist forces were about to be defeated by the Ukrainian army last summer, we saw that Putin was not prepared to let that happen, but he was also unwilling to deploy large Russian units into Ukraine to defend the separatists.

Why do he and his associates lie about having troops there and about the casualties that they have taken? Because neither foreign nor domestic audiences would be happy with the truth. Putin's actions to date do not tell us what his future aims will be. Saving the separatists and himself from defeat does not mean that he is prepared to back them as they try to take more territory. We know they want to do so. They are completely open about this. But we should not assume that Putin will pay any price to support them. We should not assume that Putin cannot be deterred. Many people think he cannot be. This is a misunderstanding.

Second, about sanctions, Putin and sophisticated Russian economists are not of one mind about the impact that sanctions have had. Some call it marginal. Others consider it significant. But no one denies that sanctions have had some impact or that over the past year Russia's economic outlook has deteriorated. The only question is whether sanctions affect Russian actions on the ground. I believe sanctions do affect policy. Putin may well hope that if fighting in Eastern Ukraine stays below the peaks it reached last year, the west will start to roll back sanctions. There are many indications of this.

But he must also know that if fighting increases, new sanctions are likely and a rollback will be impossible. It is hard for me to believe that this awareness does not constrain Russian support for separatist leaders, and we should make clear how high the cost will be of further enlargement of the separatist enclaves.

Third is the much disputed issue of whether and how to support the Ukrainian military. A sudden infusion of western arms will not turn the tide when fighting is in full swing. It might even lead Russia to escalate its own involvement. Those have been reasons that many have brought forward not to provide lethal assistance to the Ukrainian military. But the problem that the United States and its allies face now is somewhat different. Their primary goal, as I said a moment ago, is to keep the separatist enclaves from becoming a larger part of Ukraine. Our goal now should be to deter a new wave of violence in Ukraine, and in particular an effort by separatists to expand their holdings.

That is a goal that western military aid can help to achieve. Without its separatist enclaves, Eastern Ukraine will grow. The country's political and economic disintegration will continue, and Russia's involvement will increase. We have to be smart about strengthening Ukraine's army, and we have to be careful, but a Ukraine that can defend itself is essential to a strategy of restabilization. Expecting the conflict in the East to freeze itself is wishful thinking.

Finally, about where Putin will strike next. His Ukrainian policy is a threat to the security of NATO members. The alliance has been right to reinforce and reassure frontline states, and it must do more. We cannot afford the luxury of unpreparedness. All the same, as long as the Ukrainian crisis continues, my judgment is that Russian military pressure against other neighbors is remote. Being bogged down in Ukraine makes it harder for Putin to pick other fights, yet the unfolding conflict in Ukraine will surely affect his calculus down the road. If Putin emerges the victor in this conflict, if a pro-western government is kept from succeeding, if Russia's nationalist mood deepens, if the rich and powerful countries—democratic countries of Europe and the United States fail to stay the course, if this is where we end up, Putin will draw his own conclusions. The Putin we face in the future could be even more dangerous than the one we face today, both for his neighbors and for us.

Thank you, Mr. Chairman. I look forward to our discussion.

[The prepared statement of Dr. Sestanovich follows:]

THE PREPARED STATEMENT OF DR. SESTANOVICH

Chairman McCain, Senator Read, members of the Armed Services Committee: Thank you for today's opportunity to discuss Russia's confrontation with the West over Ukraine. This is a subject of fundamental importance for the future of Euro- pean— and indeed global—security.

The past year has been a frustrating one for both policymakers and policy analysts—in fact, for anyone trying to anticipate Russian moves. Time and again, many of us failed to gauge Vladimir Putin's motives. Often we thought he would be ready to unwind the crisis when he was actually about to double down. He made promises that he did not keep and created a powerful case for Western sanctions. Putin has personally antagonized European and American leaders in a manner that has few precedents in the history of Russia's relations with the West.

After a year like this, where do we stand and what should we think? I'd like to focus on four issues that have produced considerable debate. They bear directly on choices that your committee must make.

- First is the question of Putin's aims and calculations. I often hear it said that he cares more than we do about Ukraine. Because he feels that the stakes for Russia are high, he may be hard to deter.
- Second is the effectiveness of sanctions. Many say these have not worked well. Putin, we hear, will not be swayed by economic pressure; he has convinced the public that Russia must not be pushed around.
- A third much-debated issue has to do with helping Ukraine militarily. Giving arms, it is said, will only escalate the fighting—and bolster Putin's claim that the West is seeking to bring Russia down.
- Finally, a fourth fear, about where this confrontation is heading. Many people worry that Putin will turn against other neighbors, especially our Baltic allies.

There is a kernel of truth in each of these claims. But they do not tell the whole story. To develop the right strategy, we need a fuller picture.

First, on the nature of Putin's commitment: we should neither minimize nor exaggerate it. When separatist forces were about to be defeated by the Ukrainian army last summer, we saw that Putin was not willing to let that happen. But he was also unwilling to deploy large Russian units in Ukraine to defend the separatists. Why do he and his associates lie about having troops there, and about the casualties they have taken? Because neither foreign nor domestic audiences would be happy with the truth.

Putin's actions to date do not tell us what his future aims will be. Saving the separatists—and himself—from defeat does not mean he is prepared to back them as they try to take more territory. We know they want to do so; they are open about it. But we should not assume Putin will pay any price to support them.

Second, about sanctions. Putin and sophisticated Russian economists are not of one mind about the impact that sanctions have had. Some call it marginal; others consider it significant. But no one denies that sanctions have had some impact, or that over the past year Russia's economic outlook has deteriorated. The only question is whether sanctions affect Russian actions on the ground.

I believe sanctions do affect policy. Putin may well hope that, if fighting in eastern Ukraine stays below the peaks it reached last year, the West will start to roll back sanctions. But he must also know that, if fighting increases, new sanctions are likely and a rollback will be impossible. It is hard for me to believe that this awareness does not constrain Russian support for separatist leaders.

Third is the much-disputed issue of whether and how to support the Ukrainian military. A sudden infusion of Western arms will not turn the tide when fighting is in full swing; it might even lead Russia to escalate its own involvement. But the problem that the United States and its allies face now is slightly different. Their primary goal should be to deter a new wave of violence and, in particular, an effort by separatists to expand their holdings.

This is a goal that Western military aid *can* help to achieve. Without it, separatist enclaves in eastern Ukraine will grow, the country's political and economic disintegration will continue, and Russia's involvement will increase. We have to be smart about strengthening Ukraine's army, and we have to be careful. But a Ukraine that can defend itself is essential to a strategy of re-stabilization. Expecting the conflict in the east to freeze itself is wishful thinking.

Finally, about where Putin will strike next: his Ukraine policy *is* a threat to the security of NATO members. The alliance has been right to reinforce and reassure front-line states, and it must do more. We cannot afford the luxury of unpreparedness.

All the same, as long as the Ukrainian crisis continues, my judgment is that Russian military pressure against other neighbors is remote. Being bogged down in Ukraine makes it harder for Putin to pick other fights. Yet the unfolding conflict in Ukraine will surely affect his calculus further down the road. If Putin emerges the victor, if a pro-Western government is kept from succeeding, if Russia's nationalist mood deepens, if the rich and powerful democracies of Europe and the United States fail to stay the course—if this is where we end up, Putin will draw his own conclusions. The Putin we face in the future could be even more dangerous than the one we face today—both for his neighbors and for us.

Thank you, Mr. Chairman. I look forward to our discussion.

Chairman MCCAIN. Well, thank you very much, and thanks to all the witnesses for their very important comments and, frankly, thought-provoking assertions. There is a Michael Gordon piece on April 22nd: ''In a sign that the tense crisis in Ukraine could soon escalate, Russia has continued to deploy air defense systems and built up its forces near the border.'' ''This is the highest amount of Russian air defense equipment in Eastern Ukraine since August,'' Marie Harf, the State Department spokeswoman said. ''Combined Russian separatist forces continue to violate the terms of the Minsk II Agreement signed in mid-February.'' Of course we are seeing indications of renewed fighting, and there are many who believe that Mariupol is the next target for Vladimir Putin. It also seems, at least to this observer, that the price that Vladimir Putin has paid is not very high, and the benefit, at least in Russian public opinion, has been rather beneficial to him.

Mr. Brzezinski stated in his prepared statement and verbal statement, ''We should provide military equipment, including air defense and anti-tank weapons, as well as key enablers, deploy intelligence surveillance capabilities, and conduct military exercises in Ukraine as EUCOM did in the summer of 2014.'' Then in addition to that in your comments, Mr. Brzezinski, you said we should increase sanctions and have rapid response capability, and also assist other countries, specifically you pointed out Georgia.

Admiral, do you and Dr. Sestanovich agree with those comments, Admiral, or do you want to add or subtract from those recommendations?

Admiral STAVRIDIS. I certainly would not subtract at all. I agree with them. I think that just to put specificity on it in terms of the aid, we ought to be providing lethal, in particular anti-tank weapons, anti-armor weapons. That is a very visible, relatively easy to operate, and sensible system in addition to all the other UAV and so forth, things we should do. I will add one other, which is cyber. We should be assisting the Ukrainians in cyber. They are under continuous attack.

Chairman MCCAIN. Dr. Sestanovich?

Dr. SESTANOVICH. I am broadly sympathetic with those ideas. Let me mention, though, that I think in looking at the list of measures, we should focus primarily right now on steps that will increase the operational effectiveness of Ukrainian forces. I am not so sure that having exercises in Ukraine is going to do very much along those lines. I could be persuaded, but I would really want to focus on what you can do to increase the fighting capability of Ukrainian forces.

I mention this for a reason that goes beyond just the deterrence factor and the ability to resist when separatists push out from where they are. I think it also affects the internal politics of Ukraine in an important way. If the Ukrainian government cannot hold the line against separatist offensives, they will lose ground— it will lose ground politically, and the people who will gain politically are the informal militias often with, to be honest, somewhat extreme ideologies and aims of their own. That is an outcome that will be terrible for Ukraine's future. So we are not looking simply to produce a military result by offering assistance to the Ukrainian military. We are trying to stabilize and support a democratic government.

Second, I would add about sanctions. I think right now increasing sanctions is going to be a very heavy lift. The crucial aim has to be to prevent the rollback because that is actually a rather pressing danger right now.

Chairman MCCAIN. I agree, and as long as they are dependent on Russian energy, I do not think you are going to see. We forget Crimea. We forget the shoot-down of the Malaysian airliner, *et cetera*. Mr. Brzezinski, first of all, there is one other area, that is the intense propaganda campaign that Russia is waging in the Baltics in particular, but also Moldova and other countries. Do you have a response to that because I do not think, frankly, that our Radio Free Europe and other capabilities that we had during the Cold War is in the 21st century. I think it more like 20th century.

My other question is, suppose the *status quo* remains and we do not implement the procedures that you and the other members of the panel have largely supported. What do you think Vladimir Putin's next move is? Is it Mariupol? Is it Moldova? Is it areas even further?

Mr. BRZEZINSKI. Thank you, Mr. Chairman. Regarding Russia's information campaign, they are crushing us. Russia spends billions of dollars in sending out cyber messages, TV messages, radio messages. It has lobbyists all over western capitals pushing out the Russian line, some of it accurate, some of it blatantly false. We have nothing in comparison, and I actually think this is where we need to go back to the Cold War and think about lessons learned.

We actually had a very sophisticated information campaign. It was led by the U.S. Information Agency, an independent structure in the U.S. Government that actually was responsible for doing nothing but messaging, and it has separate offices in our embassies all around the world. That is the kind of level of effort that we are going to have to put into if we are going to counter this Russian information campaign, and it is a campaign that is going to have to be mirrored by our allies.

Regarding Russia's next move, my sense is that Putin is just positioning himself as an opportunist. I was struck by how his strike, unsuccessful albeit, but his strike against Mariupol earlier this year coincided with the Greek elections because he clearly knew that the west was not going to really be able to develop the consensus necessary to respond forcefully to that violation of the

Minsk Agreement. It was not going to be able to generate the consensus necessary to impose additional sanctions.

So when I look down the road, I actually think that the most likely move by Putin will occur when there is another economic crisis or political crisis in the west or in Ukraine, and Putin will move quickly to seize and exploit that opportunity. I think it will be towards Mariupol if not all the way down towards Crimea. It is possible it could be other parts of Donetsk and Luhansk.

A second contingency I keep my eyes on is Kharkiv. Kharkiv is the technological center of Ukraine famous for its aviation and aeronautics industry. There has been an ongoing campaign of terrorist attacks by Russian proxies, by Russian forces operating in that area, bombs going off in metro stops and such. So I think what is happening there is Russia is continuing to see they can soften up that region so it could become like another Luhansk.

Looking beyond Ukraine, I am less worried about a strike against the Baltics, but more against Georgia. Why Georgia? Because Georgia is a weak state. It is a small state. We have precedent in 2008 of Russia trying to take over Georgia. Also Georgia is strategically important. It is the cork that goes into the Caspian Sea of oil and gas. It is the pathway for the southern corridor that is going to bring Caspian gas into Europe. If Putin really wanted to do something strategically significant to mitigate the southern corridor, well, you take Georgia and you shut down the southern corridor that way. That is what I keep my eyes on.

Chairman MCCAIN. Thank you. Senator Reed?

Senator REED. Well, thank you very much, gentlemen. One of the issues that arises along with sanctions is the declining price of oil because of, frankly, the actions of the Saudis. I might suggest it is more powerful than formal sanctions. There are some indications—I have spoken to Dr. Sestanovich before—of the effect within Russia where there are strikes. They are building sort of. I think there is too much to suggest that we have reached a turning point, but there is some indications of turbulence because of this situation.

So, Admiral and your colleagues, comment on the effectiveness of the sanctions, but also the effectiveness of continued low oil prices.

Admiral STAVRIDIS. I think Dr. Sestanovich has it about right. They are neither catastrophic nor are they de minimus. They are kind of in the middle. Mr. Brzezinski has it right in that if you really want to get attention with sanctions, there is another level you have to go to. He mentioned a couple of things. I would throw into the mix more targeted individual sanctions at high level individuals in the Putin circle.

In terms of the oil pries, anything that depresses oil prices does, in fact, have, I think, perhaps a higher immediate effect than the sanctions. The two in combination are powerful, and I think over time will be possibly the way in which we finally get Vladimir Putin's attention.

Senator REED. Mr. Brzezinski?

Mr. BRZEZINSKI. Sir, my sense is that when we think of sanctions in the west, we have a terrible tendency to try to mirror our decision making and political processes upon Russia. You know, when Russia suffers—when we suffer a negative 1, negative half percent GDP growth, we have a political crisis. Governments fall. When

Russia suffers negative 2 or negative 3 percent growth, they look back on their history, a rich history, a proud history, of enduring great economic and military hardship: Napoleonic wars, Hitler's invasions, and such.

They have a much heartier approach to economic endurance than we do, in part because of history, in part also because of the political structure. Russia is an autocracy. It is a one-man state. Not a one-party state, a one-man state. It is much more capable of enduring that kind of hardship that comes with economic sanctions.

I have to say, if I could, that when I think about our unwillingness to impose harsher sanctions, I am very, very surprised. It is rooted very much, I think, in Europe's unwillingness to suffer the blowback that would come with those sanctions. But if you look at the economic balance between Europe and Russia, between the west and Russia, it is pretty surprising.

Senator McCain has described Russia as a $2 trillion gas station. Well, that $2 trillion gas station has one customer. It is the EU [European Union] primarily. The EU is a $12 trillion economy. It is backed by a $16 trillion economy, the U.S. economy. How is it that a $2 trillion gas station is able to intimidate an economic entity, the EU and the United States, that is 15 times its size? I think that is rooted in strategy shortsightedness, I think more fecklessness, allowing the neighbor to be invaded and doing not as much as we could. To a certain degree, corporate greed, an unwillingness to take on the financial costs of what one needs to do for moral and strategic reasons.

Senator REED. Dr. Sestanovich?

Dr. SESTANOVICH. There is no doubt that Russia is an autocracy, but I do not think we should exaggerate the stability of that system. This is a strong but brittle political order. The kinds of tremors that you referred to, Senator, with the wave of strikes, for example, are a reminder that the legitimacy of an order of that kind is always precarious.

About sanctions. They have been much more powerful than we expected because of their interaction with oil prices, just as you suggest. The effect of the oil price drop would have been less if Russian banks and corporations had had an easy option of refinancing through the west. The partial closure of access to western capital markets has made the problems of Russian state corporations and other businesses that much greater.

It is probably right, at least many Russian friends of mine say what Admiral Stavridis said. Just if you want to sharpen the impact of sanctions, the easiest option available is to add sanctions on individuals. We always think that the broader sanctions are going to have the bigger bite, but people in Putin's circle, who will see that sanctions against them are their reward for being supporters, will, you know, have to ask—whether the boss knows what is doing.

One other thing about individual sanctions is that they do not require the same degree of unanimity to have an effect. We can take actions of that sort ourselves, and that can send a powerful message about where we are going with our policy.

Senator REED. Thank you. Thank you, Mr. Chairman.

Chairman MCCAIN. Senator Rounds?

Senator ROUNDS. Thank you, Mr. Chairman. Gentlemen, thank you for your testimony this morning. I would make two assumptions, number one that the situation in the Ukrainian is not acceptable in its current way. The *status quo* is not acceptable, and that it should be reversed. The second assumption would be that the United States should not go this alone. If those two assumptions are correct, does NATO, assuming that NATO is the appropriate entity to take action, does NATO have the current capabilities to respond appropriately to the aggression that has been shown by Mr. Putin? Second of all, does NATO through the individual membership, do they have the political will to get it done? Is that what is slowing it down today?

Admiral STAVRIDIS. I think the short answers are yes and no. NATO has the military capability. It over matches Russia in essential every military area, particularly in its high tech, its number of troops, its combat aircraft, *et cetera.* But it does not—because it is a consensus-built organization, which means all 28 have to agree with anything, I think it is highly unlikely that the alliance would step into Ukraine in a significant way and respond to Vladimir Putin on the ground.

I do think if Putin came after a NATO country, Estonia being the sort of classic scenario that is bandied about, I do believe the alliance would respond strongly and aggressively to that.

Mr. BRZEZINSKI. Sir, I would second what the Admiral said fully. Let me go one step further and say that if the alliance—not the alliance. If we in the west want to do some of the things that the committee has supported, like arm the Ukrainians, and some have argued more severe sanctions, I think we are going to have to move out of institutions like NATO and the EU and go into coalitions of the willing.

That has risks because it underscores a certain amount of disunity, but it has the advantages of actually actions being taken. I am confident that if the United States were able to pull together a coalition of the willing, and I think it could, for example, in arming Ukraine, I would look to the UK, I would look to Poland, I would look to that Balts, I would look to some of the Scandinavian countries.

Canada? Thank you. That coalition of the willing could provide weapons that are needed by Ukraine. It would demonstrate that such moves are actually constructive, and it would eventually pull the alliance along.

Dr. SESTANOVICH. I would add only that we should not over focus on military support for Ukraine. Military support is extremely important, but the crisis that Ukraine faces is a much broader one. Given the severity of the economic disaster that is happening there, it is not too much to call it an existential crisis.

We can build up the Ukrainian military and still find that the Ukrainian economic order collapses. To deal with that problem, we are, in fact, going to need, as you suggest and as my colleague suggests, multilateral support. We need the IMF [International Monetary Fund] to step up as it has, and Congress should understand that what lies between the *status quo* in Ukrainian and the unthinkable collapse of the Ukrainian economy is probably going to be that institution, plus other creditors helping out. This is going to have to be a pretty broad-based international effort to rescue the Ukrainians, and it is going to be expensive.

Senator ROUNDS. Which in this particular coalition does not exist today.

Dr. SESTANOVICH. Well, I would not actually say that. The core of it exists. There has been a good IMF response, and western governments have been helpful, but it is probably going to have to draw in Ukraine's creditors. The Ukrainian Government is reaching out to try to reach understandings with its creditors so as to build up its—strengthen its balance sheet. But this is something that is an ongoing process, and I do not mean to say that the business of the Armed Services Committee is not the only element of saving Ukraine. I do mean to say that actually. I think it is important for the Armed Services Committee to understand how much the work of other arms of the U.S. Government will be crucial in keeping Ukraine afloat.

Senator ROUNDS. Thank you, Mr. Chairman.

Chairman McCAIN. Senator Manchin?

Senator MANCHIN. Thank you, Mr. Chairman, and thank all of you for being here today. I just came back from Berlin a few weeks ago, and it was the Aspen Group that met with Ukraine and Russian scholars and leaders. First of all, the thing I walked away with is the Cold War today is colder than the Cold War when we had declared a Cold War. If anybody could touch on that, how we build the relations, if there is something we did not know about or do not know about it. But seems like there is a very little conversation, dialogue trying to build any relations with the United States and Russia. First and foremost that.

Next of all, exporting oil is something we are talking about in our Energy Committee. Do we export crude? We have not done it since the 1970s with the OPEC [Organization of the Petroleum Exporting Countries] situation we ran into back in the early 1970s. Could we use this strategically for our Nation? I think it would be hard for me to explain in West Virginia that we ought to export more crude and it will make prices cheaper at the gas pump. That is a hard lift to explain. Strategically they would back it 100 percent if we knew that we were putting—bring those nations who have oil that they have used their energy for the wrong reasons. So to touch on that one.

Finally, we were told at this conference we had for a week that we should be very careful if we arm the Ukrainians, even defensive weapons, because it gives Putin really a reason to do what he would like to do anyway and be more aggressive. So they were very cautious. I took the approach that in West Virginia if a bully is picking on somebody who is undersized or taking advantage, you just want to make sure they have the ability to fight back. So I would have said let us give Ukrainian all the weapons. I have a second thought and a pause button on that one because of what I had heard, and it could just escalate things much worse than what they are today. I do not know if they will get much better, and maybe that is the only recourse we have.

So first of all, on the relationship of crude and then basically the Ukraine arming—arming Ukraine.

Admiral STAVRIDIS. I am going to go with West Virginia on the approach. I have difficulty with this argument that says we should not arm them because we will provoke Vladimir Putin. I think he has demonstrated he is the bully in the neighborhood, and I do not think acquiescing to a bully is ever the right way to go. I say that as a guy who stands a towering 5-foot-5.

[Laughter.]

Dr. SESTANOVICH. I think, second, on the dialogue with Russia, we still have zones of cooperation with Russia. We cooperate with them to some degree in counterterrorism, a bit in counter piracy. We have reasonable dialogue at the moment with the Iranian nuclear negotiation. We will see. We have also seen Russia turn around and give advanced anti-air warfare weapons. So I would say that portion of the dialogue is breaking or about to break further. But we do have some minor areas where we can continue to talk, and we should do so.

In terms of the crude oil, I think it makes sense in the broadest context of energy to try and alleviate others' dependence on Russian gas and oil, back to the $2 trillion gas station that the chairman has, I think, correctly identified. Thanks.

Senator MANCHIN. Mr. Brzezinski?

Mr. BRZEZINSKI. Sir, thank you. Regarding energy security, energy security remains a key vulnerability for Central Europe. They are very dependent upon Russian oil and gas. In Poland I think it is 80 percent, 90 percent of its oil from Russia, over 60 percent of its gas from Russia. Ukraine, of course, the numbers are much higher. The same in the Balkans. So we have to make addressing Central Europe and Europe's energy security a key priority, and I think U.S. policy has done that. We helped drive forward the southern corridor that will bring Caspian gas to Europe.

I think the next big project really should be fostering the infrastructure necessary to integrate the energy markets of Central Europe together because they all remain certain islands, separate nations, separate energy markets, and to integrate them into that of a wider European energy market. That is a key long-term project.

As for U.S. exports, I think it can only help Europe's energy security situation if we unleash our oil and gas upon the global market, but we should have also realistic expectations of how that will affect European security. Most of those exports probably would not go to Europe. They would probably go to Asia and elsewhere where the prices are higher. But by flooding the global market, it would actually push more global oil and gas towards Europe, helping diversify Europe's energy sources, and that has already been the case to a certain degree with LNG [liquified natural gas].

Regarding arming Ukraine, I stand with West Virginia without question. I look at not only is it a strategic requirement because, you know, weakness can actually attract aggression certainly when you have a neighbor like Putin, but I also look at it as a moral imperative. I have to say I look back prior to the attack and remember—the attack of Ukraine. I remember how the Ukrainians actually sent a company of their own soldiers to a NATO Article 5 exercise. They have actually sent more soldiers than we have to Steadfast Jazz in Poland and Latvia.

Then I think about the protestors on the Maidan who risked their lives, some lost their lives, expressing their desire to be part of Europe, their desire to be part of the EU, and their desire to be part of NATO. For us to kind of stand and look at our shoes in a way and limit our assistance to MREs [meals ready-to-eat] and blankets when they are being attacked by an aggressor I think is morally indefensible.

Dr. SESTANOVICH. Well, West Virginia seems to be carrying the day here. But I would say, first of all, we are not limiting our assistance to MREs and blankets, and you know that, Ian. We do need to be smart and careful here because getting involved with weapons assistance can be destabilizing. We need to make sure that is not. I am completely in favor of providing this assistance, but I think that it is silly to say there are no risks involved. There are risks, and that is why we have got to be smart about it. But the risks are very, very great doing nothing, so we have got to watch it.

About a Cold War, Admiral Stavridis is right that there are plenty of areas where we still can manage to sit across from the Russians and talk to them. But this is a real Cold War suddenly, and we need kind of strong nerves for it. The message to the Russians has got to be you brought this on yourselves, and the principal responsibility for finding a way out of it to start with is not ours. It is yours because you began this. That I think it is really quite important for us to have the strength of that conviction.

Finally, about energy, I agree with a lot of what has been said here. I would give you an operational suggestion. Secretary Kerry last summer said it is a goal of American policy to reverse—reduce European energy dependence on Russia. How is it coming? I would like some regular progress reports. I would say that is something to ask about in a persistent way to make sure that our government does better here what it does not always do, and that is follow through.

Chairman McCAIN. Well, Doctor, the risk of destabilization assumes that the situation is stable. Senator Ernst?

Senator ERNST. Thank you, Mr. Chairman. Thank you, gentlemen, very much for being here today. We appreciate your testimony. I would also like to extend my congratulations to Senator Cotton, who is not with us today. Late last evening they welcomed an addition to their family. Baby boy Cotton was born last night. Anna is doing very well. So congratulations.

Chairman McCAIN. He should be here this morning then.

[Laughter.]

Senator ERNST. Yes, her work is over, at least for the time being. Anyway, I would like to shift just a little bit and talk a little bit about Turkey just while I have you here, Admiral, if we could. It seems to me and to many others that Turkey has been maybe not such a strong ally as they should have been. We see that ISIL and al-Nusra seem to have extensive lines of communication within Turkey, and I would contend that there are those within the administration that tend to turn a blind eye to those types of activities going on within their own country.

So, Admiral and others, if you could address Turkey and the situation as it stands with these different terrorist organizations.

Maybe what the United States and others could do to discourage this type of activity.

Admiral STAVRIDIS. Senator, thank you. There is some good news in the overall stature of Turkey in the Alliance, and we should remember that. I am going to criticize Turkey momentarily. But we should remember that in every NATO operation—Afghanistan, Libya, the Balkans, counter piracy—Turkey has been there. They have sent troops. They have been very engaged and involved. What is happening now, you are absolutely correct, is a different story. Despite having obviously a lengthy and extensive border that abuts both Syria and Iraq, among others, they have, in my view, failed to step up in the anti-Islamic State campaign. They should be much more involved at every level beginning with open access to their bases, more intelligence sharing, more use of their military capability against the Islamic State up and including ground troops, which I think are inevitable against the Islamic State. So in all of those dimensions Turkey is falling short.

The reason is they are conflicted about objectives. They really want to see the end of the Assad regime. The Islamic State is nominally fighting the Assad regime. They have failed to recognize that the greater danger at this moment is, in fact, the Islamic State, A, and B, we can do both of those things. We can see the end of Assad and defeat the Islamic State. It requires will, coordination, cooperation. Turkey needs to do more.

Senator ERNST. Gentleman, any other input?

Mr. BRZEZINSKI. I guess the only thing I would add, and I completely agree with Admiral Stavridis' points about what we could be expecting of Turkey. Also I think we have to take into account Turkey's perspective in its relationship with the west, which I think has caused it to kind of, to a certain degree, and I do not want to overstate this, disenfranchise itself, particularly within the European community. It has been frustrated now by over a decade of basically a cold shoulder from the EU and its aspirations. So, it has been almost kind of let free to a certain degree, and it is pursuing, not surprisingly, a more independent policy. Our challenge is how to pull Turkey in a constructive way fully into the fold.

Senator ERNST. Very good.

Admiral STAVRIDIS. May I add one point? It is simply that we should give Turkey credit for dealing with an enormous humanitarian challenge. There are 2 million Syrians who are being—the bill for whom is being footed by Turkey, and that is a contribution to humanity. It does not, in my view, diminish their shortfall in reacting militarily.

Senator ERNST. Thank you. If we could turn back to Ukraine and Russia just for a moment. We have talked extensively today about arming the Ukrainians, and I take the West Virginia approach also, very much so. But are there other types of programs that maybe we could assist the Ukrainians with? We have talked about, of course, energy. Are there agricultural programs, other types of things where we can just continue to assist them and build up their own economy in the meantime?

Dr. SESTANOVICH. Well, Ukraine could be an agricultural powerhouse rivaling the greatest Midwestern producers. So watch it.

Senator ERNST. Yes, they could.

Dr. SESTANOVICH. Watch out what you wish for.

[Laughter.]

Surely the failure to develop Ukrainian agriculture has probably been as big as any failure of the past 25 years in sort of unlocking the potential of the Ukrainian economy. The Ukrainian economy is in such terrible shape that almost anything would help. The good news is that you have a team in place in Ukraine that really gets it, that understands what needs to be done. It is not as though we need to go there and tell them have you thought about Ukrainian agriculture. They know what the potential is and they know what the problems are.

They need the resources. They need the political will. They need the time to let some of their measures take hold. But they are pretty serious about what they are doing, and they are implementing the kinds of policies that make some of them nervous actually about the political viability of it. That is why the prime minister calls himself a kamikaze appointment. He figures he ultimately is going to go up in flames. But I think the most important ingredient in this is time. They need to be able to hang in there long enough for the measures—the very sensible and path-breaking measures that they are taking to have some effect.

Senator ERNST. Great. Thank you very much. Thank you, Mr. Chairman.

Chairman MCCAIN. Senator Shaheen?

Senator SHAHEEN. Thank you, Mr. Chairman, and thank you all very much for being here. Most of our discussion this morning is focused on Russia, which is the elephant in the room. But as we look at threats to Europe's security, how concerned should we be about the economic situation that particularly parts of Europe are facing, the rise of nationalist parties in some of the—Greece, Spain, some of the other countries of Europe, and the potential for that to provide fertile ground for ISIS and terrorist attacks and Russia to agitate in a way that is a threat to European security? How do you assess that with respect to what is happening with Putin? Anybody.

Mr. BRZEZINSKI. Senator, I think you have hit on an underlying foundation element of Europe's security situation, and that is the fragility of its economy. The fragility of its economy is contributing to some of these emerging kinds of nationalist xenophobic parties. They are certainly not constructive.

When I think of how this relates to Russia, I watch very much what is going on in Greece because I really feel that that could have a powerful impact on the European economy. There is a Grexit. There are going to be shutters, and they are going to go particularly through Southern Europe. It could even push Europe back into a recession.

A Europe that is back into recession is a Europe that is going to be less able to mobilize as a whole to take on the challenges that we are discussing today, be it Russia's aggression to the East, be it the extremism we see in the Middle East, the extremism we see in North Africa and the refugee flows. It is going to be harder for us to act as a transatlantic community in a unified way. I really believe that I think Putin watches this closely. I think he times to a certain degree his moves according to when he thinks the alliance, the community, the transatlantic community, will be least able to respond forcefully and cohesively.

Senator SHAHEEN. So what more—I am assuming that, Admiral Stavridis and Dr. Sestanovich, that you both basically agree with that assessment?

Admiral STAVRIDIS. I do. If I could just add, I think this is an area where we mentioned earlier that Putin was crushing us in the social networks and strategic communications. The Islamic State is crushing us as well.

Senator SHAHEEN. Right.

Admiral STAVRIDIS. We need a countervailing strategic communications focus there along with all the other things that Ian has talked about. I think it is extremely concerning.

Senator SHAHEEN. So that is what my next question was going to be. What can we do to better shore up what is happening in those areas? Obviously a better social media information campaign that can help respond. What else?

Admiral STAVRIDIS. The economic piece is enormous here, and I would start with the T–TIP, the Transatlantic Trade [and Investment] Partnership that is coming. I think that is a way that we can help the European economy directly. Putin hates it because it ties Europe to the United States, and I think it would have a very salutary effect.

Thirdly, we ought to continue to do within the military domain the NATO things that you know so well, Senator. I think there is no single point solution here, but we need to continue to be engaged militarily, politically, economically, and in a communications sense. Otherwise, storm clouds ahead.

Dr. SESTANOVICH. Could I just add one kind of encouraging word about——

Senator SHAHEEN. Please.

Dr. SESTANOVICH.—you know, these bumbling, passive——

Senator SHAHEEN. Encouragement would be helpful.

Dr. SESTANOVICH.—spineless, underperforming Europeans as we tend to portray them. Putin does watch this carefully, but he exaggerates the impact of it. That is why he has been so surprised by the extent of the European reaction to what he has done in Ukraine. He thought this would basically be forgotten within months. His view has been the European cannot tie their shoes. They cannot do anything collectively. In fact, the European Union has regularly reaffirmed a sanctions policy that Putin never saw coming.

It gets me to the question of marketing because what you need from marketing is a good product. The most important part of developing a consistent public relations line is having a unified policy. So far we have been pretty good at that, and I think if we can hold that we have the solid foundation on which to build a more effective marketing policy. But the crucial ingredient, and I think this is—this hangs in the balance over the next 6 to 8 months is to keep a policy across the board—military, economic, political support for Ukraine. That can unravel. Putin may not turn out to be totally wrong about the disunity of the west. But if by the end of the year he looks up and discovers that actually he has not been able to divide Europe and the United States, that will be a powerful message for him.

Senator SHAHEEN. So when you say ''we,'' you are talking about Europe and the United States together.

Dr. SESTANOVICH. I am, yes.

Senator SHAHEEN. Okay. Thank you, Mr. Chairman. I have other questions, but I will——

Chairman MCCAIN. Senator King?

Senator KING. Thank you, Mr. Chairman. I am going to be a bit of a contrarian here and try to create an alternative scenario. I am trying to figure out whether this is the Sudetenland in 1938 or Sarajevo in 1914, and bear with me for a minute.

Putin has a very weak economy. Domestically everything stinks. He has got an 80 percent approval rating in Russia principally because of nationalism and his strong man image of standing up to the west. Is it not possible that arming the Ukrainians, which would obviously be public in some way, shape, or form, whether it is anti-tank weapons or something else, would be playing into hands? It would be—he would say, see, I am standing up against America. They are trying to invade our region of the country—our region of the world. They are putting their troops and arms—maybe not troops, but arms, and it would embolden him.

The second piece of my question is, you guys, it seems to me, are assuming a static universe. We arm the Ukrainians and nothing else happens. He would obviously respond in some way, and he is sitting on the side of the poker table with most of the chips because this is on his turf.

I guess to throw one other historical analogy into the mix, Cuba. We were willing to take the world to the brink of nuclear because of perceived Russian, not aggression, but placement of weapons in our sphere of influence off of our country. I think we have got to think and put ourselves in his shoes, and I am just concerned. I have not made any firm decision on this, but I just do not think it is as easy as you say.

We arm the Ukrainians. Then what happens? That is my question. Mr. Brzezinski, do you want to tackle that one?

Mr. BRZEZINSKI. First, I would say that arming the Ukrainians is not the sole answer. I think it is a critical element of a strategy.

Senator KING. But what does he do if we arm the Ukrainians? What is the next—it is not just going to be, oh, they armed the Ukrainians. What does he do next? What happens next?

Mr. BRZEZINSKI. If he moves further into Ukraine after we arm the Ukrainians, the Ukrainians will impose higher costs on the aggressor forces, on the Russian forces. I think that is going to be—

Senator KING. But he controls the media in Russia. Does he care—I mean, he is not responsive. As you said, if your economy went down 1 percent we would have, you know, people in the streets. Over there they are not even going to know that there are more troops dying in the Ukraine.

Mr. BRZEZINSKI. You know, again, it is not the sole answer, but if there are more Russians, to put it crassly, dying in Ukraine, I think it is going to cause a political problem for Putin. One thing that I have been struck by watching this crisis politically or this even in Russia, is the steadfast, earnest, determined effort of the

Russian Government to cover up Russian deaths in Ukraine. They do not have the equivalents of Faces of the Fallen. They deny that anyone has died. They deny their forces are there. They intimidate families who have lost their sons or their daughters in Ukraine telling them to be quiet. They move them out of their homes. They threaten to take away their death benefits. It is really interesting—

Senator KING. So is it your position then that we arm the Ukrainians and Putin does not respond. There are no further weapons for the separatists. There are no further troops. I mean, this is a fact—in fact a status universe. We arm—there is no response. I find that impossible to believe.

Mr. BRZEZINSKI. No, what happens is that, one, the Russians face a more complex situation, a more lethal situation. They face the prospect of a prolonged and costly conflict. That, I think, will probably deter them trying to push further in Ukraine. It also might make it possible they would be more willing to back out of Ukraine, at least out of Eastern Ukraine. It would also demonstrate to Putin the west is serious about sustaining the post-World War II security order, that we are not going to tolerate unilateral revisions of orders by force. I think those are dynamics that we are not trying— we are not leveraging, and we should be leveraging.

Senator KING. Others have thoughts about my question? I hope you appreciate that this is not easy.

Admiral STAVRIDIS. I totally do, and I think the key word Ian used was ''probably.'' This is a——

Senator KING. Yes, I heard that word, too.

Admiral STAVRIDIS. This is a calculus just like any decision you make, particularly when you use lethal force in any dimension. We always say in the Navy, when you release ordnance, everything changes. You are taking a gamble. But my assessment is that this is the right choice. In terms of what happens, I think Putin then has a much harder choice. He can either bring Russian forces under their flag into Ukraine and face, I think, overwhelming world approbation, or I think at that point he does start to unwind and reaches for the frozen conflict solution. I think that is probably the best we get out of this.

But, no, of course, it is not static, Senator. There will be changes, and it is a risk, and it could go very badly. But I still recommend that we do it.

Senator KING. Sir?

Dr. SESTANOVICH. Senator, since I am the member of the panel who has expressed the most unease about this, let me try to bring you around to my way of thinking about it since I do support it. I think you mentioned a static universe. You should not assume that the universe is static as long as the United States does not do anything. This is a fluid situation right now in which separatists are trying to push out in all directions, whether it is along the coast, to the north, to the west. They only control about a third of Donetsk Province and half of Luhansk, and they have said they want it all.

They are definitely going to try to get the rest of these provinces, and they are going to try to expand their control across along the coast. It is just a certainty. I mean, if there is anything that one can regard as a law in this universe, that is going to happen. So the question——

Senator KING. I certainly understand that there are risks on both sides. There is a risk of inaction, and the universe is not static in either way. I do understand that. I am just trying to assess the risks, the relative risks.

Dr. SESTANOVICH. The best scenario in which to try to have some effect of bolstering the operational capabilities of the Ukrainian forces is when there is a lull. The fact that Putin has agreed, even while not abiding by it much, but there is something of a lull. That is the moment in which we have to try to make sure that when people start to challenge that lull, to push out from what they hold now to what they want to hold, that they will be stopped, that they will face more resistance.

I mean, the thing that finally makes me think, yes, of course you have to support these forces is without greater capability, there is no way that the separatists are not going to push out. So here is the question I would put to you, and I think you should put it to people in the administration because they plainly do not want to do this. What is your plan for stopping the separatist offensives that are going to go, you know, west, north, and south from the land that they hold now? What is your theory of the case?

Senator KING. Right.

Dr. SESTANOVICH. If you have got a theory of the case that enables the Ukrainian forces to hold the line, great, you know. Let us hear it. I think if there were such a case that could avoid the——

Senator KING. The risk.

Dr. SESTANOVICH.—the uncertainty and the risk that you identified, great. I just do not think there is that. But I would say challenge people in the administration because my sense is from your—what you said, that you do not want that to happen. I think they do not want it to happen either, but I do not think they have any answer to how they are going to keep it from happening.

Senator KING. It seems to me the answer is that we have to game out what happens in both directions. Particularly I am concerned, as I expressed, that when you are playing chess with a Russian, you had better think three moves ahead, not just react and no reaction, and I think that is a very important point. I am sorry, Mr. Chairman, I have gone over, but a very important point that we also have to game out the results of doing nothing, and see is there a strategy or is the strategy just to not act.

Dr. SESTANOVICH. Gaming it out and doing nothing is totally easy. The separatists will expand their territory.

Senator KING. Thank you. Thank you, Mr. Chairman.

Chairman McCAIN. Well, I think, Doctor, you have just answered my question, and I would ask the other two witnesses, and I am sure I know the answer. Is there any doubt that there will be attempts and, for no reason to believe they are not going to be successful under the present scenario to expand the Russian influence through the separatists throughout Ukraine? Admiral, is there any doubt in your mind?

Admiral STAVRIDIS. None whatsoever, and I suspect sooner rather than later. I think the mortars and the artillery are shelling the villages outside of Mariupol right now.

Mr. BRZEZINSKI. I completely agree with the Admiral. It is going to happen.

Dr. SESTANOVICH. I think the separatists are determined to have this happen. What we do not know is how much the Russians really want it to happen. I think the Russians are unwilling to let the separatists be defeated, and the game that is going on between them is the separatists want to push out, and then when there is a counter response, they want to say to the Russians you have got to defend us. You have got to keep us from losing any of the ground that we have taken. So what our interest is is to make sure that they cannot actually take new ground because once they do, that will draw in more Russian support.

Mr. BRZEZINSKI. Could I follow up, sir?

Chairman MCCAIN. Sure.

Mr. BRZEZINSKI. Actually I get very concerned about what I feel is a tendency to exaggerate the gap between the separatists and Moscow. I never saw—was able to observe any significant separatist movement in Eastern Ukraine prior to this invasion. I firmly believe that ''the separatists'' are not separatists. They are an extension of the Russian polity. They were sent in to destabilize Eastern Ukraine. They were led by Russian provocateurs. They were backed by Russian soft [power], and they were ultimately backed by Russian conventional forces.

So it is not really—there is not a tension that we can really exploit between separatists and Moscow. They are one and the same. It is an external invasion of Ukraine.

Chairman MCCAIN. I would also add that apparently if I were Vladimir Putin, and I do not pretend to understand him totally, but it seems that you achieve a degree of success, and that becomes the *status quo*. Things quiet down, then Europeans talk about relaxing sanctions and trying to find that out, and things are quiet for a while. Now, at least according to General Breedlove, we are starting to see an increase in activities after a period of lull. It seems to me that that has been pretty successful so far for Vladimir Putin. Doctor, is there anything to that theory, do you think?

Dr. SESTANOVICH. Putin thinks he has got more endurance than the Europeans do and than the Americans do. You are right. As I said to Senator Shaheen earlier, his gamble is that whatever miscalculations he has made and how much greater the resistance has been, we will crack first. So, that is the test for us is not to crack first.

Chairman MCCAIN. Thank you. Jack, did you want to——

Senator REED. I just have just a brief comment. I think as has been indicated by the panel and particularly Mr. Brzezinski, that Putin is an opportunist. If there is an opportunity, he takes it. But he is also—I think, his timing is influenced by things like the Olympics. I think he was very reluctant to get involved in the Ukraine while the Maidan Square demonstrations were going on because he had another audience he was playing to. He was the world leader.

I think similarly at his juncture we might be having a lull because they are in the process of celebrating the end of the Great Patriotic War, and he wants everyone to come and pay homage to him, *et cetera*. But after that, which is within a few weeks, there is no more, sort of him personally, reason to hold back, so that might be a factor also.

But I think, and I will go in a second, I think your point, Doctor, which is this becomes ultimately a test of wills against this individual. He has the advantage of being an individual. We have a collective will we have to sustain and hold together. Thank you, Mr. Chairman.

Chairman McCain. I do not mean to prolong this dialogue too much longer, but it seems to me energy is still a key item. We could develop within a couple of years an ability to get energy from the United States over to that part of the world, which I think would have a significant impact. That has nothing to do with arms or weapons. Finally, could I ask if there is an agreement on that, Admiral?

Admiral Stavridis. I agree with that, Senator.

Mr. Brzezinski. Sure.

Dr. Sestanovich. Absolutely.

Chairman McCain. I thank the witnesses for a very——

Senator Shaheen. Mr. Chairman, can I——

Chairman McCain. No. Yes.

[Laughter.]

Senator Shaheen. Can I ask a couple more questions?

Chairman McCain. Absolutely.

Senator Shaheen. Thank you. I want to go back, Dr. Sestanovich, to your comment about providing lethal weapons because I think there is a lot of agreement on this committee that we should provide those weapons, but you said we have to do it very carefully. So you talked about doing it during the lull. What other things do you think we should be doing as we are looking at providing those weapons to do it carefully?

Dr. Sestanovich. Training is crucial. Intelligence capabilities are crucial. Those are the two that would come to my mind right off the bat. Then of course the economic backdrop means that we have to make sure that while we are getting those Ukrainians in smart formation on the front lines in good looking new uniforms, and knowing their tasks, the home front does not just collapse. That is—you know, if there is anything that is more desperate than the military outlook, it is the economic outlook.

Senator Shaheen. Yes. I certainly think that is pretty clear to this committee. But let me ask because one of the things that I think that you all have alluded to is the importance of acting unilaterally with the United States and Europe, being united in our approach to the crisis. One of the reports about the European reaction to lethal weapons is that they do not support that, and that, therefore, this could be a potential area where we would disagree in a way that might have an impact. So how do you assess that as you look at the need to provide weapons? Admiral?

Admiral Stavridis. Disagreement within NATO is unknown terrain at all, Senator, as you know quite well from your deep experience in NATO. Think back on the Libyan operation where we saw a group of nations leaning forward, very, very involved, a group of nations supportive, and then some who were essentially opposed, but willing to kind of come along. I think that is how this would play out.

I do not accept the argument that this would somehow shatter the Alliance. I think at the end of the day you can do it within a NATO context with the Nations who want to, or as Mr. Brzezinski has said, you could create a coalition of the willing. He listed some states. I agree with that. I think there are mechanisms to deal with that argument.

Senator SHAHEEN. Any other—Mr. Brzezinski?

Mr. BRZEZINSKI. Yes, I would like to make two points, Senator. First, I would add to the Admiral's list of how coalitions fell together into NATO without collapsing the Alliance. Missile defense is an example. Iran sanctions is another. I have two words of caution on strategy for arming Ukraine or two things we need to think about is, one, I think it is important that we avoid incrementalism.

I am a little bit worried that our administration and our European allies' approach is first we will do some MREs, then we will do some Humvees, then we will do some counter-artillery radar and such. I think that is a mistake because I think that just maps out to Putin were the future is headed, and that actually will encourage him, embolden him to act while he is most effective, has the power balance most in his favor in Ukraine.

Then second, I think we would be naïve to assume just arming the Ukrainians and the Russians will not do anything. They are going to counter react. So we have to have a plan that goes beyond just arming Ukraine, so that if we provide good, robust security assistance to Ukraine, we are prepared for a sudden Russian offensive. For example, one step half-cocked and ready to go is really harsh economic sanctions that would be driven in either by the EU or by coalition like-minded nations to hit the Russians and then know in advance this is going to happen if they all of a sudden try and counter react aggressively to an effort to provide more needed security assistance to Ukraine.

Admiral STAVRIDIS. If I could, I would add, Senator, cyber. We need to add that to our shopping list as we think about how to help the Ukrainians. Thanks.

Senator SHAHEEN. Thank you. I want to switch topics for my time that is left because one of the things that happened last week is that European regulators imposed antitrust charges as Gazprom. Do you think that is going to have any impact on the energy situation?

Dr. SESTANOVICH. Yes. It has been a principle of Russian policy that Europe does not get to impose its rules on its energy trade with Russia. The result has been that Gazprom has had a very advantageous negotiating position with all European customers. It has been able to insist on separate negotiations with all customers with the result that its prices across Europe vary dramatically according to that bilateral relationship.

For Europe to say we care about our policies and we are going to enforce them in our energy trade would be of immense importance. Europe has done that in kind of tentative ways, for example, with respect to energy transportation and pipelines. It has managed to block the Russian South Stream Pipeline by saying this does not meet our rules. The Russians have time and again laughed at that and said, oh, no, those rules are not in effect because we can buy off this or that individual customer or transit country.

If the Europeans are going to turn around their energy relationship with Russia, they have got to start enforcing their rules, and it is has got to go beyond transportation. If it gets to the issue of negotiating about pricing, there will have been an energy revolution, so that is fundamental. But as you surely know from having EU events, one announcement does make a policy. The Europeans have opportunities for many procedural hurdles, reversals, and so forth.

Senator SHAHEEN. Thank you. Thank you very much, Mr. Chairman.

Chairman McCAIN. Senator Ayotte?

Senator AYOTTE. I want to thank all of you for being here. You know, having been to Ukraine twice last year and having had the privilege of overseeing the presidential elections, you know, I am just wondering, are we at a tipping point because many of us have been calling, and on a very strong bipartisan basis, for providing, you know, the lethal support for Ukraine to defend itself, as well as economic assistance, as well as increased NATO support, additional sanctions.

At some point, I mean, I have just—it is really appalling to me. It is hard to express how I feel about it because we have been in almost uniformity here in the Congress on this, on things that, you know, we do not always agree on, so many things. On this we have sort of on a bipartisan basis thought this was the right thing to do, and I am just worried.

Are we not at a critical moment where—I feel like in having listened to—I was at the Munich Security Conference having listened to, for example, the Germans speak about their objections to providing lethal arms. It is almost like I feel like that in some ways Ukraine is being written off, and I hate to be so cynical about it.

But if we do not act soon, where is this going? I mean, is there not a huge urgency for this? I thought there was an urgency last May. But can you help us understand how urgent is this situation where you are—you know, we have got Ukraine with the economic situation, and in addition having to defend their territory.

Admiral STAVRIDIS. I think we are at a critical point, and I think what will happen in the next two to four weeks, maybe the next two to four months, is going to be another bite out of Ukraine by the separatists. I am hopeful that that will be the tip that pushes us over to come in with not only the lethals, but really the entire package of things we have talked about today.

As of yesterday, as I mentioned to the chairman, mortar and artillery fire at the villages outside of Mariupol. That is what you do first when you soften up for a land advance. We may be there now. We will know more in the next couple of weeks. We have to get going on this if we are going to have impact.

Senator AYOTTE. I just wanted to also follow up. One of the things that struck me about this whole thing, and just correct me if I am wrong in my thinking, and it has really bothered me in terms of our foreign policy from the beginning, and that has been the Budapest Memorandum. It seems to me that we are not stepping up to help provide this kind of assistance that we have talked about here. We signed this agreement. As we look at, for example, even the context of Iran, other goals that we have of nuclear nonproliferation, does this not in the big picture undermine—I just still do not understand why other countries would want to give up their nuclear weapons when their territory is invaded, and yet we—you know, our signature on that memorandum seems to mean nothing in this context. Are you worried about that in the picture as we look at our larger foreign policy here?

Mr. BRZEZINSKI. Senator, I agree with you. I think there are two important issues at stake here in the violation of the Budapest Memorandum. I was a volunteer in Ukraine working in Kiev when that was signed, and I remember the impressions in Kiev intimately. It was celebrated in Ukraine as an affirmation of the west's commitment to its independence and its sovereignty. It was even seen as an affirmation of its attempts to become a European—an integrated member of the Europe ''Community of Democracies'', because they were giving something up that was recognized as kind of potentially very important to their own security, nuclear weapons.

Now 25, 30 years later, we are in a situation in which that Memorandum has been blatantly violated. Every country around the world that has or is aspiring to weapons of mass destruction is looking at it very carefully. What are the consequences if you give up such aspirations or such weapons? Well, you become more vulnerable? Will someone back you up? Not necessarily clear that they would.

Then I think it is a real hit to the west's credibility because it was really seen a document driven by the United States and Great Britain, Europe and the United States. That is what the Ukrainians back when I was there in 1994 were looking to for assurances. Not to Russia, but to the United States and to Europe, and they are not getting it. It has really undercut our standing, the credibility of our security commitments.

Dr. SESTANOVICH. Senator, I agree with you, but if it does not loom large in my thinking it is because it seems to me the case for supporting Ukraine is so strong.

Senator AYOTTE. Right. Well, it is compelling.

Dr. SESTANOVICH. No matter what.

Senator AYOTTE. I mean, it is compelling.

Dr. SESTANOVICH. Yes. I do not think we should in any way have the view that if there had been no Budapest Memorandum, we would be less interested in this case, or that we would be less interested in other cases where there is not that same issue.

You are right that the commitment of the United States has been shown to have been made perhaps without full thought as to what we really meant by it. But I think—to me it is not the central issue. The broader question is the interest that we had in the entire order that we were trying to create in Europe after the Cold War.

This is—the reason this is a fundamental threat to that interest has less to do with the disposition of Soviet nuclear forces. The truth is the Ukrainians did not really want to keep those things, and it has much more to do with more fundamental considerations of war and peace and our future relations with Russia.

Senator AYOTTE. Well, I hope—I know my time is up, but I know how dedicated the chairman has been to this issue, and how passionate he is, and I share his passion for this. I hope that—I hope that the administration is listening to the testimony of all of you today. Thank you.

Chairman MCCAIN. I want to thank the witnesses for being here today. It has been very helpful. The meeting is adjourned.

[Whereupon, at 10:51 a.m., the committee adjourned.]

www.ingramcontent.com/pod-product-compliance
Lightning Source LLC
Chambersburg PA
CBHW081801280526
45789CB00008B/2950